Birdies

Way up in the sky, the big birdies fly.
Way down in the nest, the little birdies rest.

With a wing on the left and a wing on the right,
the little birdies sleep all through the night. SHHHHHHH!

DON'T WAKE UP THE BIRDIES!!!!

Then up comes the sun; the dew falls away.
"Good morning! Good morning!" the little birdies say.

Way up in the sky, the big birdies fly.
Way down in the nest, the little birdies rest.

With a wing on the left and a wing on the right,

the little birdies sleep all through the night. SHHHHHHH!

DON'T WAKE UP THE BIRDIES!!!!

Then up comes the sun; the dew falls away.
"Good morning! Good morning!" the little birdies say.